Y0-CQB-646

EMERGE

The Power of Your Purpose

BETH STEWART

Endorsements for
EMERGE

"Scripture tells us that, 'Where there is no vision the people perish.' Our modern life and culture has flooded our eyes and ears with possibilities, but anesthetized our hearts to the primary purpose of our creation. God is awakening a new generation of single minded people who have chosen to pursue God with all their hearts. Beth Stewart is one of those people, and her book *Emerge: The Power of Your Purpose* is full of practical guidelines to help you discover the point of your creation. God made you and he has many purposes to fulfill through your life. Don't allow one more day to go by without a sense of god's divine purpose in your life. I encourage you to read Beth's book and pursue your purpose today!"
Joan Hunter, Author/Healing Evangelist, JoanHunter.org

"I recommend this book to anyone looking for a true and meaningful purpose in life."
Marcus Mecum, Senior Pastor, 7 Hills Church, Florence, KY

"*Emerge* is a terrific book that will help you find, understand, and operate in your purpose."
Jennifer Minigh, Owner, Shade Tree Publishing

BethStewartMinistries.com

In *Emerge: The Power of Your Purpose,* Beth provides practical insights and encouragement to help you receive a fresh vision for your life and scriptural guidance to help you find your God-given purpose. Beth also provides keys to living your life to your fullest potential and to fulfill what you are on this earth to do. *Emerge* will prove that when you are on the path of your God-given purpose in life, you will have great power to be fulfilled in your own life and to help others, as well. You'll discover treasures in God's Word to help you stay on the path of your destiny, and you'll learn that when you align your priorities with God's Word, His plan for your life will begin to unfold. You are destined for greatness!

God designed you for a purpose, and it is His will for you to find it, walk in it, and achieve your highest potential.

EMERGE:
THE POWER OF YOUR PURPOSE

Beth Stewart

Copyright @ 2017 Beth Stewart Ministries
Print ISBN: 978-0-9909447-4-4
e-Book ISBN: 978-0-9909447-5-1

Scripture quotations marked NIV are taken from the HOLY BIBLE, NEW INTERNATIONAL VERSION®. Copyright © 1973, 1978, 1984 International Bible Society. Used by permission of Zondervan. All rights reserved.

Scripture quotations marked KJV are taken from the King James Version. The KJV is public domain in the United States.

Scripture quotations marked NLT are taken from the New Living Translation®. Copyright © 1996, 2004, 2007 by Tyndale House Foundation. Used by permission of Tyndale House Publishers, Inc. All rights reserved.

Cover Art by Heather May Photography.

The purpose of this book is to educate and enlighten. This book is sold with the understanding that the author and publisher are not engaged in rendering counseling, albeit professional or lay, to the reader or to anyone else. The author and publisher shall have neither liability nor responsibility to any person or entity with respect to any loss or damage caused, or alleged to have been caused, directly or indirectly, by the information contained in this book.

Visit our Web site at BethStewartMinistries.com.

I dedicate this book to my mom in heaven, who mentored me to follow the ways of Christ and to use all my gifts and talents for the kingdom of God and for the good of His people.

CONTENTS

FOREWORD

I am so honored to recommend this book to anyone looking for a true and meaningful purpose in life. As senior pastor of Seven Hills Church in Florence, Kentucky and pastoring thousands of people, the most common question asked is "what is my purpose?" Many of my sermons that I have preached have been on the topic of purpose as I believe this is a need that all people long to fulfill.

The Power of your Purpose would be an excellent tool for leaders to help people understand not only their purpose, but how it empowers the whole body of Christ and in your personal life as well. I must admit that I may be one of the best candidates to write the forward of this book because of the constant questions I receive as a pastor pertaining to this subject. Seven Hills church is a strong believer in small group studies and fellowship and this would be an excellent tool for any small group discussion. We also minister to many more in our Freedom night services to help with addiction recovery. Many addictions begin with people who feel as though they have no purpose. Directing them to a purpose is what most of the people need to begin their pathway to recovery.

According to the New Testament online bible concordance, the word purpose is found fifty-six times in the King James version. If it was important enough to be written in God's Word, then it is important for us to address this issue. There is more to your life story than what we see and know. We are born to progress and live on purpose. Beth has combined not only how to find your God given purpose, but how walking in your purpose empowers you throughout your life. Her stories are honest and real and will surely inspire you to begin seeking your purpose and destiny. Her personal experiences with the Holy Spirit are shared with great wisdom to help the reader relate to a life of real meaning. She has poured her heart and soul in the words that will forever change your life.

My life drastically changed at the age of sixteen when I gave my life to Jesus. My life changed again a year later when Jesus gave me a glimpse of my purpose. Both experiences have been a life long journey to fully understand; however, my life has never been aimless since those two unforgettable moments. Far too many people never invest in knowing their "why;" the fact you're reading this forward lets me know you will not be one of them long.

You were made to matter and this book will also help give you the practical biblical thought provoking steps to destiny. *Emerge: The Power of Your Purpose* will embolden you to influence others with a lasting impact.

This is a must read for any person who has ever struggled to find their God-given purpose or passion, or ever doubted that they had anything of value to offer this world. With a style that's straightforward and practical and most of all wise, Beth will help you navigate the confusion of your own heart to uncover and unleash your influence in a way that is beneficial not only for you but the world around you as well.

Marcus Mecum

Senior Pastor, 7 Hills Church, Florence, KY

PREFACE

Have you ever wondered why you have been placed here on the earth? I'm sure you have, and I truly believe that all human beings at one time or another ask the same questions: *Why am I here? What is my purpose? Where did I come from? Where am I going? What is life about?*

No matter how you started out in life or how bad your life may have been, you are not a mistake. God would never have allowed you to be born if you had not been included in His universal plan. You are essential.

You are not an accident, either. You were creatively and thoughtfully woven together by your Creator. Your Creator has an incredible imagination, and He took the time to carefully think about each intricate part of your being. The way you look and talk, your personality, and all your other traits are a part of God's own creativity.

There is no need for you to wander through life simply trying to stay busy. Each generation seeks meaning and a reason for living. Many people live and die without ever really knowing their purpose.

I have talked to so many people in this life, and when I ask them about their purpose in life, they usually answer by giving me their job title. But what if they lose their job? Is their purpose lost, too, then? Purpose is not necessarily the job you do, even though it can be attached to that. Your purpose is actually who you *really are* at the core of your soul. Deep within the chambers of every human heart, regardless of your race, heritage, or socioeconomic status, is the longing to know why you are here. Whether you are conscious or unconscious of this, we all are searching for identity. One of the deepest cravings of the human spirit is to find a sense of significance in this life. In other words, we want our lives to make sense.

I remember my mother once made a monumental remark to me shortly before her passing. She looked up at me and said, sincerely, "You know, Beth, one thing I have learned about life is that it is one strange experience." My mother always had a wonderful sense of humor. I couldn't help but laugh, even in that solemn moment. I have since thought many times about her statement. I knew she had seen many historical events take place in her lifetime. She was alive at the time of the assassination of President John F. Kennedy, she married a man who had fought in World War II, she had lost a friend in the conflict in Vietnam, she had lost her parents when she was fourteen, and so on. I frequently reminisce about what she said that day, and I have pondered the truth in her words: "This really has been one strange life." Many things and events that happen in our lives just don't seem to make sense, and most questions we have will never be answered on this side of eternity.

One thing is for sure, however: We are all searching for the meaning to life. Many tragedies result from this unanswered question. Attempted suicides, murders, theft, and serial killings are all mostly birthed from humans searching for a sense of identity; unfortunately, some people believe this will bring them a sense of significance.

Some people try to find meaning in the accumulation of wealth, in social status, or in material possessions. However, most of us know that this is not the answer to the longing of the soul for purpose. I personally know many wealthy people who are very unhappy and many poor people who are extremely content. I have a very good friend who has little in terms of material wealth; nevertheless, she has the happiest marriage and is always full of joy in her relationship with Christ.

The only thing worse than dying is living without purpose. You may be wondering about this thing called purpose and how to find it This is exactly what we will explore together through this book. *Emerge: The Power of Your Purpose* will take you on a soul-searching journey into the reasons for your very existence.

God designed us all for a purpose, and it is His will for us to find it, walk in it, and achieve our highest potential.

WHAT IS PURPOSE?

Everything God created has a particular purpose. Nothing exists for itself alone, but everything is related to something else. Let me give you some good examples. The sun and the moon were each created for a purpose. Both provide light, and yet they each rule at different times: One rules at night and the other rules during the day. A battery has a purpose for a car, a car has a purpose for people, the key starts the ignition, the wheels help the car move, and so on. You get my drift. Everything and everyone has a purpose, and each purpose is significant.

You have a purpose and a task to complete on this earth. You are a necessary part of the world's population and a vital link to your generation. We all need your contribution. You are important.

Purpose Can Seem Big or Small

When we think about God creating someone for a purpose, our minds may consider the following characters in the Bible:

* God purposed Noah to build an ark and save the world from the flood (see Genesis 6–9).

* God ordained King David's son Solomon to build His temple long before Solomon was born (see 2 Samuel 7).

* God determined that a virgin girl would give birth to the Savior of the world (see Isaiah 7).

* God appointed Paul to be a messenger to the Gentiles (see Acts 9).

All of these biblical examples may seem big to us, and yes, not everyone is called to be the leader of a country or to save the world from a hunger crisis; however, it's not important how big or small a person's purpose seems, *your purpose is important!* If God took the time and energy to create you, then you are important to His bigger plan. Don't ever think that your purpose on this earth is insignificant.

Helping people is probably the most overlooked and underestimated purpose that a person can fulfill. When we help someone besides ourselves, we may think it is small, but to the one receiving our gift of help, it can be a very big deal—and anytime we help others, it *is* a big deal to God.

Without Purpose, Life Has No Meaning

All of us ask questions like these: *Who am I? Why am I here? What was I born to do? What can I do to make a difference in my world? Why am I different from other people?* These are universal questions to human beings from all walks of life and all places on this planet.

The world is a place in which stress, depression, and hopelessness is on the rise. People seem to have lost their sense of purpose and have lost touch with their sense of basic values and morality. When a person loses their sense of morality, they begin a downward spiral, and they lose sight of God and His purpose for their lives. You see, God intends for each of us to live by His standards, and not simply follow our own compass in life.

History shows that the value and quality of people's lives decrease when they lose their sense of identity and purpose. When there is no purpose, people tend to lose self-control and they no longer have any moral convictions. Having no ethics or moral standards only makes matters worse. When guilt and condemnation slip into the soul, the search to a darker and deeper place is begun. Where there is no purpose, there is no demand for discipline.

After trying out many avenues of sin, the soul eventually will ask, *Is this all there is?* One of my relatives is a prime example of someone who has asked this question. She was well into her seventies and had lived without Christ for most of her adult life. I can remember when she fell sick and she spoke the very words that many people speak at the end of their lives when they haven't followed any sense of purpose. She simply asked, "Is this all there is to life? Is this it?" I never forgot those words, as I found it a very sad statement for a human being to make, to find the meaning of her life to be so insignificant at its end.

You may be asking this same question. The good news is that it's never too late to discover your purpose. You can begin today to put meaning back into your life.

Purpose Is Found Only in the Creator

Until we discover our purpose, our lives will lack the very heartbeat of significance. We must first realize, however, that discovering our purpose is dependent on us. God has already done His part by creating us for His purposes on this earth. It's now our job to search out and fulfill that purpose. To become who and what we were designed to be and what we were born to do, we need to connect with our Creator. This is essential and the most fundamental principle in discovering our purpose.

We will never know the answers to all our questions while we live on this side of eternity. Our heavenly Creator is the only One who knows all the whys and hows of things. Although we certainly have the right to ask for wisdom and understanding, we still may only know in part after He does answer us. Thank goodness that He has provided a user manual (i.e., the Bible) for our lives to help us fill in the gaps.

Think of a manufactured item. If you wanted to know the purpose of a certain product, whom would you ask? The manufacturer, of course. Most products come with an owner's manual that describes how the item works, that instructs the owner on its proper use and maintenance, and provides troubleshooting tips and toll-free numbers to call for help.

When we have questions about our lives and why we were created, we need to ask our heavenly Manufacturer for help and information. He knows what our purpose is, because He is the One who designed us.

Purpose is the key to life. Everything and everyone has been created for a purpose. Our purpose explains and reveals the meaning of our lives' experiences and demands, and it provides a perspective that gives significance to our lives.

God designed you for a purpose, and it is His will for you to find it, walk in it, and achieve your highest potential.

YOU WERE MADE
ON PURPOSE

The Bible says that before the Lord formed us, He knew us and set us apart.[1] His eyes saw our unformed bodies, and all the days ordained for us were written in His Book. When He created us, He knit each of us together in our mothers' wombs, to be fearfully and wonderfully made.[2] We are His handiwork, created to do good works, which He prepared in advance for us to do.[3] We were made on purpose *and* for a purpose!

We Are One of a Kind

It's obvious in life that we are all different. No one of us is the same, and neither is any creature on this planet exactly alike. Likewise, despite the trillions of snowflakes in a single storm, there are no two alike—then or ever. Take a moment to think about that and realize how awesome God is! He is creative beyond measure. Imagine living on earth for a thousand years and never once experiencing all the creative images of God. Think about all the animals, the ocean creatures, the insects, and the people. Look at the cultures, the races, and the personalities of each member of the human race. We are all unique. Each one of us is one of a kind. Nobody else can be you, and you can't be anybody else. I must be authentically me, and you must be authentically you.

According to the Merriam-Webster's online dictionary,[4] being *authentic* means "conforming to an original, so as to reproduce essential features" and being "true to one's own personality, spirit, or character."

I remember when a friend of mine was somewhat perturbed with my ways of thinking and doing things. Keep in mind that I wasn't doing anything sinful or wrong, but I was just different from her. She said to me in a quite agitated voice, "You're just Beth!" I can still see her sneer when she said it. My answer to her was simple: "Well, I don't know who else I'm supposed to be!" Suddenly, instead of looking like a snarled-up sourpuss, she looked like a deer caught in the headlights of an oncoming car. Yes, I was just being Beth! I believe the reason she was so stunned was that because, deep down, there is no other answer to someone who is being authentic.

We are who we are, imperfections and all. No one can live life exactly like you can. God is far too creative to make duplicates.

Many people are unhappy because they don't know who they are, and so they try to imitate others who seem to have it all together. This never works. We cannot be the one-of-a-kind persons we were created to be if we are constantly trying to be someone else. Personally, I would rather be true to myself than worry about rejection. I once heard a statistic that said that when speakers go before a large audience, before they even open their mouth, one out of every ten people in the audience will automatically not like them. Imagine that! Before we even speak, people are judging us. If there is nothing we can do about that and we didn't cause it, then why should we waste our time trying to change their opinion? It's time to get over the fear of other people's opinions and move forward in the authenticity we have in God. The world is waiting for us and for what we can bring to the table. Likewise, we must be sure to show grace to others who are walking in their own authenticity, even when we don't understand it.

God Doesn't Second-Guess

God never creates things just for the fun of it. He always has a purpose in mind. Not once when He was creating a person did He say, "Uh-oh," or "Let Me try that again." If you read the book of Genesis, you'll see that after He created anything on this earth, the Bible tells us, "And God saw that it was good." And, in fact, after He created mankind, He said that it was "very good."

Because God is a God of purpose and because everything in life has a purpose, each of the creatures on this planet has a God-given purpose. You might wonder how a cockroach, a snake, a mosquito, or any other seemingly disgusting insect or creature could have a purpose. But God took as much time to create those creatures as He did to create the beautiful butterflies and the colorful birds. Just because we have a personal dislike for something, that doesn't mean it has less value or more of a purpose than anything else.

Our ignorance of something's purpose doesn't mean that a purpose does not exist. It simply means that we don't understand God's thinking behind the purpose of it yet. In the same way, you might not understand your own purpose yet, or that of someone else. You might look at other human beings with a critical or judgmental attitude, because they don't behave like you think they should. That still does not diminish their purpose. We tend to judge things according to our own backgrounds or fears, but thank God that He sees things differently than we do.

We may be tempted to second-guess God's purpose for our lives, perhaps because of some past mistake or due to a general lack of self-esteem, but God does not second-guess His purposes for us, and neither should we.

Seeing Life from God's Viewpoint

The way you think and see your life will shape the future you will live out.

Let me ask you a simple, yet profound and life-altering question: How do you define life? Your perspective on this issue is important, and it will ultimately define how you spend your resources such as time and money and how you choose to value your relationships. Your thinking *does* matter.

What image do you have of yourself, your future, and your self-worth? Do you think it's possible or impossible for you to achieve your dreams? Do you tell yourself that you've tried to pursue your dreams, but that it just didn't work out? One of the most important aspects of achieving all you were meant to be is changing your view of your life to match God's view. His view is always bigger than ours, and it is always much better.

The Bible teaches us that the Lord's ways are higher than our ways, and that His thoughts are higher than ours. I choose to allow Him to hold the best way to solve a matter or to answer a prayer. Yes, it can be frustrating at times, because our human mind wants to figure things out on our own. However, our human minds are very small compared to our living, creative God, who can see our lives from *every* angle and from every aspect of time. He wants us to bring our viewpoints up to a higher level of the life He has called us to live.

Not Envying the Lives or Purpose of Other People

Now, come on, let's be honest—haven't we all envied someone else's life at some point?

As humans, we naturally like to follow the lives of others. This is one reason that social media has been so successful. We all know people who spend untold hours each day scrolling down through social media feeds, just to see what other people are up to. I've been guilty of doing this myself, but I also realize that the lives that people portray on social media aren't always real. Take this next story for example.

An acquaintance whom I was following on social media consistently uploaded pictures of her and her husband. The pictures were of their travels, their fun adventures, and their loving family members, and it would give me warm fuzzies and convey a sense of their strong and wonderful marriage. I was convinced they were a "perfect couple"—until one day when I discovered that their marriage was in jeopardy due to infidelity. I then realized that all the wonderful posts that this woman had made were probably just a front to make other people believe that everything was perfect, when, in fact, it wasn't at all. I learned that day not to envy other people's lives, especially those we know nothing about, because people can put on any front they desire.

In addition, envy robs us of contentment. It drives us to think we need more money, fame, beauty, talent, or power. It will keep us focused on the very things that will steal our joy and peace, ultimately leading to frustration, fatigue, and failure.

Envy is a trap that can keep us from becoming all we were meant to be. If we are always preoccupied with what others are doing, we will miss what God is doing in us, and we will try to be something we were never meant to be. Let's face it—it's hard work being someone else, and most of the time, everyone else can see right through our façade but us. But when we discover our awesome self through our unique relationship with our heavenly Father, we will see that He loves and accepts us exactly the way He created us to be. He adores us. It's foolish to compare ourselves with others, because we are actually incomparable.

When thoughts of envy try to creep into my thought life, I simply tell those thoughts to go away. It is a choice, and I choose not to go there. Also, we must learn to celebrate the success of other people. Instead of being jealous of others' promotions or their good fortune, I remind myself that if God did it for them, He will also do it for me! It took time for me to develop that attitude. But now I am genuinely happy to see other people succeed because it gives me hope for my own future. Another tool I use to battle envy is to reflect on all the life events through which God has brought me. I can celebrate my own personal successes and progress instead of envying the success and progress of others.

God created us on purpose and for a purpose. It is His heart's desire that we become all that He has created us to be. It's time for us to stop second--guessing ourselves and envying others, and instead strive to see our lives the way that God does.

God designed you for a purpose, and it is His will for you to find it, walk in it, and achieve your highest potential.

WHAT IS YOUR PURPOSE?

I live in the Greater Cincinnati area with my wonderful husband and two awesome sons. The rest of my extended family live back in my hometown of Flatwoods, Kentucky. It wasn't until I had my first child that I realized how much I missed having my extended family around. I tried to continue working, but when my second child arrived a few years later, things became too challenging and something had to give.

I found a precious lady in my area who was more than willing to help us with the boys a few days a week. I had interviewed several ladies, and Mrs. Glover was perfect for us. She was a wonderful Christian woman who had a lot of experience taking care of the elderly and children.

One day, I was preparing to speak at an event, and my topic was the same subject as this book. As Mrs. Glover was preparing to leave my house, she asked what I was speaking about. I explained to her that I was hoping to help people find their purpose. Without hesitation, she replied that she already knew *exactly* what her purpose was. I must have had a look of shock on my face—mainly because the majority of the people with whom I talk have no idea what their purpose is. When I probed her further about her statement, she said, "I have always known that I was put on this earth to help other people who can't help themselves. I have sat with the elderly, the handicapped, children, and many others who needed help. I am the happiest when I am helping others. That is how I know my purpose." Wow! How powerful! If only everyone could learn their purpose with certainty, what a different world this would be.

How to Find Your Purpose

When searching for your purpose in life, your first step must be to seek God and pray. This is just the beginning, but as you pray, study His Word, and pursue Him, I believe your purpose will unfold in a beautiful way.

As you commune with God and search your inner self, be sure to write down your thoughts and revelations. Not only will these notes help you to discover your purpose, but they also will help to reaffirm it during seasons of doubt.

Remember that you don't need to see the whole picture just yet, especially because that picture may evolve. Also, you may adopt different roles when changes take place in your life. Ask yourself, "What should be the center of my life? And am I pursuing a job, a career, or more money—or am I seeking my real purpose?"

After you pray and seek God, your next steps include taking a self-inventory of your skills and talents. The discovery of your purpose is really the discovery of you.

Your Talents and Abilities

Many people fail to realize that God not only created us for a purpose, but also that He gave us many talents and abilities, as well, and your purpose is tied innately to these. Some are recognizable at an early age, while others are to be discovered throughout your life.

Your purpose will not require anything from you that God has not already prepared for you. God never requires more from His creations than what He has already built into them. Just as a manufacturer would never expect anything from the product that it wasn't designed to do, neither does God require anything of His creation or His creatures that He didn't build into their lives. Apple seeds are not required to produce strawberries. Likewise, the seeds God has placed in your life are designed to produce what He wants to bring forth in you.

The Bible includes many examples of God giving people certain natural talents. He filled Bezaleel with wisdom, knowledge, and skills to create all the necessary artistry for the tabernacle.[5]

Both of my two sons, Alex and Austin, have an innate aptitude for music that showed up at a very young age in their lives. I quickly understood and recognized these gifts, as they oozed out in every opportunity the boys were given. They would bang on boxes, plates, tables, and any other object they could find. I'll admit that this drove me crazy at times, but I patiently tried to allow their gifts to flow out of them unhindered. Even now, as my adult children, Austin plays the drums in a children's church group, and Alex has a roomful of instruments he consistently plays. Those were natural gifts that they had been given the ability to cultivate. God provided these talents, but it was up to them to use their gifts for a greater purpose.

Our talents and abilities include not only natural ones, but spiritual ones, too. The Bible says that every person has received a spiritual gift.[6] Some have the gift of faith, some have the word of wisdom, others have gifts of helps or teaching. There are many others; the gift itself is not the issue—using what you have been given is! I know that one of my gifts is teaching, and so I use every opportunity to teach that comes my way. It might be helpful for you to take a spiritual gift test to identify your gifts. Keep in mind that you will probably have more than one. The Web site giftstest.com provides a quick and easy online test that you can take, but there are many others online, as well. Find the one you feel most comfortable taking, and discover the gifts that you can use for the good of others. Make a list of both your natural and your spiritual gifts and talents as you learn what they are.

Your Likes

You should inherently like what you are supposed to do. If God didn't put the gift within in you, then you would never have the desire to do it.

Think about all your favorite things to do, and write them down. It might be picking out flower arrangements, organizing dinners, or even cooking those dinners. Everything you enjoy is worth examining, because these are likely your greatest strengths and what you are the most good at doing. For example, if someone enjoys planning and executing employee orientations, this could mean that they have a gift for professional development, and this could fulfill their purpose of helping others find and reach new levels of career achievement.

When we truly become engrossed in what we enjoy doing, we tend to lose track of time. At one time, I had a job where all I could do was watch the clock and lament about how slowly the time ticked by. I couldn't wait to get out of the humdrum of each monotonous workday. That, obviously, was not a job where my talents could soar, let alone a place where I could fulfill my purpose.

Make a list of the situations in which you quickly lose track of time, then ask yourself what it was that you loved about those assignments and what kept you engaged to such a degree.

Your Passions

Passions are what drive people toward change, and they frequently include themes such as halting injustices like human trafficking, world hunger, or abortion; helping those in need such as the elderly, shut-ins, or children with special needs; and benefitting causes such as the arts and humanities or education.

One of my passions is leading people out of darkness. When I spoke on the radio each day in Cincinnati, Ohio, I received so many emails telling me how they could hear the passion and enthusiasm in my voice. People continuously commented how refreshing it was to hear someone so excited to talk about Jesus. I know exactly why they said that—because it is true! Part of my purpose is to teach

God's Word and share all the goodness that God has shown me in my own walk of faith. He set me free from depression and darkness and brought joy into my life. When I learned the ways of Christ, I began to experience a greater freedom and a newfound purpose for my life. And I now get no greater enjoyment than when I'm sharing all this knowledge and understanding with others.

Make a list of your passions, what you feel the most strongly about. If you could make any kind of difference in the world, what or where would it be?

Your Dreams

We all have dreams, and I believe God places them in our hearts to fulfill us, not to frustrate us. Our dreams may change throughout our lives, but it's important to know that each dream we have is meant to be fulfilled. Our dreams and aspirations are as unique as we are. I have learned to pay attention to the tug in my heart that alerts me to what my dreams may be.

One of the dreams I had after high school was to attend college and become a teacher. In my book *Dreams Never Expire*, I tell the story of how my dad experienced a miraculous surge in his business at the exact time when my college education was to begin. I had prayed and asked for the funding, but I had no idea how the revenue would manifest. It seemed impossible—but God is the God of the impossible, and He came through for me. I attended college and have also received my master's degree. Since that time, I have thoroughly enjoyed my career, which has provided so many blessings for my life. Only God could have brought this to pass.

You must always have hope that your dreams will come to pass. It doesn't matter what happened in your past or how your present may currently appear. God has a plan for you, and He obviously isn't finished with you yet. Learn to persevere and vow never to give up. Plow through any disappointments, heartaches, and obstacles. Stay focused on your vision and your dreams, and remember that there is no expiration date for your dreams to be fulfilled. Maybe it won't happen in the timing for which you are hoping, but God's timing is perfect. He is never too late and He is never too early—He is always right on time.

Your Life Experiences

Life experiences can be brutal, and we all deal with negative situations. Maybe it's rejection, the death of a loved one, divorce, abuse, or addiction. Life experiences can make us or break us, depending how we deal with them. One of the greatest gifts that God has given us is the power of choice. We can choose to allow our heartaches to destroy us or we can allow them to make us stronger. We can choose to emerge from our cocoons to become a beautiful, colorful butterfly, meant to be a blessing to the world.

Our life experiences shape who we are. Without the heartache of my own past, I don't believe that I would have ever truly sought God with my whole heart. But when I sought Him, I found Him, and beauty began to be formed from my ashes. One challenge in my life was my relationship with my sister, who struggled with addictions. I loved my sister to the moon and back, but I was shattered to watch the addictions change her. But in spite of all the heartache of that part of life, I have used my pain to help bring victory to others who are struggling with this same issue. I wrote the book *Addicted to His Presence* in honor of my sister. The book is currently helping other people as I travel on speaking tours about finding victory through Jesus as we learn to enter His presence.

It's important and necessary for us to go through life events that make us stronger. We must learn to love others and find compassion for other people through our own pain. Without the pain we have experienced, we never would have acquired the empathy or the sympathy we need to love. Jesus said that the greatest of all gifts is to love. This is crucial to our walk on earth—and especially our Christian walk.

You are an overcomer, and the fact that you are alive and reading this book right now bears witness to this truth. Make a list of the life-altering experiences you have made it through successfully—and remind yourself frequently that you are an overcomer!

Purpose Involves Serving Others Instead of Ourselves

You were never created to just eat, breathe, or simply take up space. I often ponder why there are so many self-help books on our bookshelves. Although they might have some good pointers in them, most of these books do not teach us how to live to be a blessing to others. The exact opposite of what they teach is true when pursuing His purpose and making it your goal in life: You are created to serve God and serve others., and that is the only place where true fulfillment can be found. When we truly find our purpose, we will realize that self-centeredness is very unfulfilling and serving is actually our joy.

We all will give our lives to something else—whether it be work, pleasure, fame, or the pursuit of wealth. I'm not saying that any of these passions is necessarily wrong, but I am saying that pursuing them will not bring fulfillment unless it's done for kingdom purpose.

Think back to the previous section, in which you took a personal inventory, and consider all the things you listed. These gifts have not been given for your personal benefit, but they are for the benefit of others. Take a moment to note how each of your talents and skills might be used to help and serve others and therefore bring glory to God.

Circumstances Can Lie

The enemy will sometimes try to trick you into believing that your circumstances control your life, dictating what you can and cannot do. This is a lie, and in order to find our purpose, we must recognize it as such.

<u>Your Past Is Not Your Future</u>

As you pursue your purpose, always remember that God is not hindered by your past. He may use your past as part of your testimony, but it can never abort your calling or your purpose.

God will use everything you have experienced for your good when you surrender it all to Him. In fact, God turned a murderer into a deliverer named Moses.[7] He also turned a prostitute into a preacher—the Samaritan woman whom Jesus met at the well.[8] Nothing you have done will every disqualify your purpose, nor will it cancel your destiny.

I personally believe that most people struggle with their past more than anything else. If our past were to determine our future, we would all be in trouble! Having faith means believing that God has a great future in front of us, and that He uses our past to help shape us for our future. We simply need to learn how to get in step with Him.

The Scriptures teach us to focus on the bigger prize.

> I don't mean to say that I have already achieved these things or that I have already reached perfection. But I press on to possess that perfection for which Christ Jesus first possessed me. No, dear brothers and sisters, I have not achieved it, but I focus on this one thing: Forgetting the past and looking forward to what lies ahead. I press on to reach the end of the race and receive the heavenly prize for which God, through Christ Jesus, is calling us.
> —Philippians 3:12--14 (NLT)

I love these verses because they remind me that we all have the same challenge: to forget our past. However, these verses also teach us exactly how to achieve victory in this area: Forget what lies behind and reach forward to what lies ahead! Let me ask you this question: How do *you* handle *your* past?

We often have feelings or attachments to the past. We sometimes don't want to let go of the good—or the bad. We tend to hold on to guilt, condemnation, and the things that have been done to us. It's true that we can't change the past, but we can learn to let it go and learn from it. The danger is in dwelling on our past. If we want to become all that God intends for us to be, we must let go of bitterness, regret, guilt, and anger from our past, and we must do what the Scriptures tell us to do and press on.

Current Circumstances Don't Determine Your Purpose

Our circumstances may help or hinder our purpose, but they will never determine our success. History provides us with many examples to prove this. Here are several of my favorite rags-to-riches stories—of people who did not let their negative circumstances dictate their futures.

Walt Disney was one of the most creative geniuses of all time. Each of our childhoods would have been so dreadfully boring without him. Can you imagine if Walt had never fulfilled his purpose during his lifetime? Our childhoods would have been so much different, with such less color and excitement. Walt Disney started out by drawing pictures for his neighbors for money, and also by being a cartoonist for a school newspaper. He went through a jobless phase in which no one would hire him, so his brother actually had to help him with a job search. Eventually, Disney landed different jobs that he used to pay the bills while he went on to animated his own cartoons. And we now enjoy the amazing gifts of Walt Disney to this day.

Steve Jobs, the founder of Apple, is now practically a household name to most of us. Jobs had been given up for adoption by his biological parents, then he became interested in electronics after his foster father showed him the joys of technology while tinkering in their garage. As a young adult, Jobs had to drop out of college because his foster parents couldn't afford the tuition anymore. He used to return Coke bottles for money and live on free meals at a local temple. His skill with technology started in a small home garage, and he eventually became the CEO of Apple, Inc.

Oprah Winfrey was born to a housemaid and a coalminer, and she definitely didn't grow up in any kind of luxury. Instead, living a life of poverty, she wore dresses made from potato sacks and often suffered abuse from family members. She entered the media world after landing a job as a newsreader at a local black radio station. After that, she got her first job as a talk show host in Chicago. After that, there was no looking back for Oprah, who is now famous, no longer the poverty-stricken child she once was.

Billy Ray Cyrus, a famous country singer and actor, is from my own hometown of Flatwoods, Kentucky, and a former high school classmate of mine. Billy had a passion for music, even back in high school, and he played in many local talent auditions. He was raised in a very humble environment. Upon graduation from high school, he tried for many years to make it in the music industry, with no success. I remember him personally telling me how he had been traveling to Nashville frequently, but how he couldn't really afford to keep doing that. His perseverance eventually paid off, however. He went on to record multiplatinum-selling albums, and he starred in the television shows *Doc* and *Hannah Montana.*

I shared these stories to remind you that your past and your current circumstances in life will not define your future purpose. If you study the lives of these people, whether you like them or not, their purpose has affected millions of lives. Whether big or small, your purpose is meant to bless others and to impact this world, regardless of what your current circumstances look like.

Change Is Inevitable

Oh, how most of us loathe change. Nevertheless, no matter how old or young you are, change is coming your way.

Change is evidence that we are alive, and it brings the realization that nothing on this earth lasts forever. We change as we grow older, when we have children, and when our children grow up. We change schools, jobs, careers, and locations. Everything is in constant change, and unless we learn to change along with it, we will become stuck in a rut. If we are inflexible and closed off to change, then it will be harder to see the new things God has for us.

We need to learn to flow with the changes in life in order for our purpose to unfold.

Our purpose can change and evolve as we grow older, so we must stay flexible. What my purpose was thirty years ago is not my purpose today. When my youngest child became an adult, that was a shocking change for me. My entire purpose shifted. I had to reevaluate my purpose for a new season in my life and begin to pursue a new journey. This took lots of soul-searching, prayer, and wisdom.

Sometimes when we discover our purpose or when our purpose shifts, our friendships can also change. Values, circumstances, moves, and changes in priorities can cause a separation (either temporary or permanent). A prime example of this can be one's salvation. When a person first accepts Jesus into his life and begins seeking His ways and His values, that person's relationships are affected—especially the negative ones that may need to be left behind. This doesn't mean that the new Christian is better than the other person whose friendship they are leaving behind; it simply means that a shift has occurred and perhaps God has new influences and connections for them to make. As difficult as this adjustment may be, it's crucial to move on with the change.

It's not healthy to think that life will always remain the same. Change promotes growth, creativity, and fulfillment.

It has been said that people initiate personal change only when the pain of remaining the same exceeds the pain of change. Boy, isn't that the truth! However, when people get sick and tired enough of being stuck in their negative circumstances, they will eventually embrace change.

My husband, W.C., is excellent at handling change. He attributes this ability to having worked in the financial business for over thirty years. He's always telling me that it's critical to embrace change if you want to succeed. Laws change, compliance guidelines change, and clients' needs change.

If we want to succeed in life, we must embrace the needed changes for our lives and fulfill our purpose. God uses change to advance, and sometimes reveal His purposes in our lives. King Solomon, the wisest man who ever lived, said it best: "There is a time for everything, and a season for every activity under heaven." We could also read these words like this: "To everything there is a season, and to every season there is a purpose."

Testing and Trials

Life here on earth is a series of tests, whether we like it or not. All creation is tested in its faith, obedience, trust, love, integrity, and loyalty. When we look at words such as *trials*, *temptations*, *refining*, and *testing*, we find that they occur more than *two hundred times* in the Bible! Character is developed by tests, but the good news is that God will allow us to retake these tests over and over until we pass them and develop the character He requires from us.

I was a schoolteacher for many years, and I have administered so many tests that I eventually lost count. Almost all of these exams were one-time tests, in which the student would either pass or fail, based on the knowledge they had retained. I'm so glad that our character tests are not like that. I know that in my life I have failed many of God's tests, but I still find myself in situations where I am tested once more to help develop my character.

Our destiny is bigger than we can imagine, and we must have the right character to be able to handle our purpose with humility; otherwise we will continue to be tested over and over again.

Our gifts and talents can carry us only as far as our character has been developed. When I am promoted to a higher position, one that carries more recognition, I sometimes ponder the trials that I encountered along the way to get to that place. I am always grateful for the tests that prepared me for my purpose in that endeavor. I realize that without the tests, I would not have been capable of handling the big plans God had for me. In fact, those plans could have destroyed me if I hadn't been ready for them. If our purpose involves lots of admiration from other people, then God wants to be sure we can handle this adulation in humility and without hurting others. The Bible says that a person is tested by the praise he receives.⁹ Sometimes God will allow people to be drawn to us so that we can love and encourage them or impart wisdom to them; He doesn't do it to build up our egos.

God can use unexpected changes, delayed promises, unanswered prayers, persecution, rejection, and other events that you're thinking of now that were huge trials for you. One of the hardest tests for me is when I have to trust God even when I don't feel Him or see any evidence of Him moving in my life. One explanation for why this occurs may be found in the book of Hezekiah.

Hezekiah was a king of whom the Bible says, "God withdrew from Hezekiah in order to test him and see what was really in his heart."¹⁰ Hezekiah had enjoyed a close fellowship with God, but at a crucial point in his life, God left him alone to test his character—perhaps to reveal a weakness in his life or to prepare him for something even greater than what he had been experiencing.

When God is testing us, we must yield to Him, humble ourselves, and seek to pass the test. Some tests are overwhelming, and we may feel as though we will never pass them; others are small, everyday tests that we simply need to work out ourselves. Regardless of how big or small our tests may be, God always has our best interests at heart and He ultimately has a great plan for our lives. Go ahead and embrace the test—pass it so that you can move on in life.

One of my biggest, and most frequent tests has been how I react when people mistreat my children. I have never minded how people treat me, but the mama bear I didn't even know existed in my heart surfaced after my children were born. On occasion, I literally shocked myself at what I was capable of doing and saying when people didn't show my children what I considered to be justice. When I look back on it now, these situations were utterly ridiculous. The very thing that drove me crazy as a teacher and that I had always criticized highly, I was now doing myself. Yes, I became one of those demanding and obnoxious parents at times, asking for special privileges for my children as if they were the only child in the class. I was tested over and over again in handling these situations. I wish I could say that I passed this test quickly, but sadly, it took me a while. One day I finally came to the realization of what I was doing. I asked God to help me overcome the anger I had that was associated with this issue. Eventually I passed that test and what a glorious day that was. I knew in my heart that I was passing, not because the injustices had disappeared, but because I now handled the people who had committed those injustices in love.

We will experience tests until the day we die. They are necessary to develop the character needed for us to find and fulfill our purpose. If you continue to be tested in a particular area, take note, because it could be hinting at your purpose in the next season of your life.

To find our purpose, we must consider many things like what we enjoy doing, what we feel strongly about, what we are good at, what we have experienced in life that could help others in the same situation, what we possess (i.e., finances, connections, time), and so on. In addition, God may use change and testing to develop us.

If you are searching for your purpose, be patient, because the revelation of your amazing self may take time. Remember to use all your talents to glorify Him and His name. D.L. Moody, a famous evangelist and author, once said that "the world has yet to see what God will do with a man fully consecrated to Him." Will you be that man or woman today? Will you be the one who uses all their talents and abilities to glorify God's name? I know that I might not be there myself yet, but I am going to try my best to be that person.

God designed you for a purpose, and it is His will for you to find it, walk in it, and achieve your highest potential.

EMBRACING YOUR AUTHENTICITY

It is important for us to embrace who we were created to be. We must be authentic.

Being Authentic

Let's talk a little more about authenticity. Being true to yourself takes a lot of courage, and it's not for the faint of heart. When we choose to be real, we open ourselves up to vulnerability. Let's be honest. Nobody appreciates rejection, and we all desire to be liked. But being authentic takes us to a deeper layer of our souls, which most of us have hidden because of past hurts, as we all tend to expose only the parts of ourselves that people have responded to in a positive way.

One lady once told me that she was very authentic, and that it had actually cost her two jobs. After a little probing into the scenario, I quickly realized that she was being more *obnoxious* than *authentic*. Being opinionated and speaking one's mind is not necessarily being authentic.

Most of the time when I speak at events, people tell me how real and refreshing I am. I believe they find me refreshing because they aren't used to people being real with them when they speak. Most people are scripted and attempt to mimic other popular speakers. Being around a lot of church folks, I see so many wannabe ministers with mild and subdued personalities trying to scream and shout like another well-known preacher whom they highly esteem.

When we are authentic, we do take the risk of people not accepting us. Our insecurities can cause us to become phony. Some people see a popular person and decide that if they could just act like them, then they would be popular, too. It doesn't work that way. First, we can't fake being another person forever, and second, we will never be happy while trying to be someone else.

I know there are many judgmental people in the world; however, when people confide in me their fears of what others are thinking about them, I always tell them to stop worrying, because those other people are usually not thinking about them at all. The basic truth is that most people are inherently narcissistic, consumed with thoughts about themselves and not others, and because they spend so much time thinking about themselves, they think others are thinking about them, too, when chances are, the other people are thinking about their own lives! People usually have too much going on in their own lives to be dwelling on what we think or feel. They might have a fleeting judgmental thought, but it's usually pretty short-lived. It's foolish to think that so many people are spending all their mental energy judging us. So, go and be free from the fear of people's opinions.

Our desire to be real and genuine must be stronger than the possibility of our being rejected. Eventually some people will get to a point where they have dealt with so many issues in life, they finally don't give a hoot what others think. Hurrah for them, but unfortunately that is not where the majority of people are at in life. You have to admit that we all respect those who have the courage to stand up and be genuine and authentic. These are the people who will try new things in life and not worry whether it's perfect. They tend to be the ones who take risks and step out in faith more, because they aren't worried whether people will think of them as failures. They simply don't care what you think. They have decided to live life to the fullest and be all they were called to be.

You'll never reach your fullest potential until you embrace your authenticity and be the person God created you to be. To do this requires you to worry less about what others may or may not be thinking.

The Masks We Wear

I remember a lesson I once taught titled, "No More Masks." I carried a mask with me and would hold it up to my face whenever I pretended to feel fear, sadness, vulnerability, or insecurity. I could be anyone I wanted to be behind my mask, and I wouldn't take it off until I was alone, where I was safe from criticism.

We all wear masks in some way or another. The masks we wear at work and the ones we wear to social events are different. The masks that some people wear are like personas; maybe a person wants to portray a different personality to a different group of people. When we are in the presence of a different group of people or even people of importance, we tend to put on a different mask for that occasion.

Let me give you some examples of masks. As I give you these examples, try to identify, if you can be brutally honest with yourself, some of the masks you may have used in the past or even currently use.

First, there's the I'm-a-great-person mask. Have you ever seen someone wearing that one? I know I have. Then there's the uber-successful mask, the I-don't-need-anybody mask, the politically correct mask, the joker or class clown mask, the know-it-all mask, the spiritually-proud-lover-of-everyone-and-everything mask, the cynic mask, the hero mask, the I've-got-it-all-under-control mask—and the list goes on and on.

Why do people wear masks? Most people wear them to protect themselves from scrutiny, or worse, rejection. We all want to be accepted by others; it's just a basic human need. Some of us handle rejection better than others, but we all must deal with it from time to time. When I taught elementary school, I used to cringe at the rejection the children would show one another even in the early years of kindergarten. They were extremely blunt about it, too. I witnessed exclusions to birthday parties, cafeteria seating issues, playground rejections, and so on. It was heartbreaking to me, because I understood the ramifications and the long-term effects. I watched outgoing children suddenly become withdrawn and shy when they became aware of their rejection by their classmates. I watched them learn to how to put on masks.

Although many people may or may not be aware of the masks they wear or why they wear them, they undoubtedly feel the weight of them. It takes a tremendous amount of energy to try to be someone you're not, and it can drain you to your core. Wearing a mask is like living a lie, and carrying that weight is burdensome. In addition, hiding behind a mask will add loneliness and feelings of isolation to your already-heavy load.

Even authentic people still slip on masks from time to time, but the number of both the masks and the occasions when they are worn become fewer and fewer. As people discover and accept their new identity in Christ, and then evolve into the person whom God wants them to be, their masks will no longer be useful or desired.

It is such an awesome feeling to throw aside the masks that beset us. I highly recommend that you give it a try if you haven't already. At first it may take great courage to be yourself, but in the long run, it's worth it. As you start shedding the masks, it may feel a little awkward at first, but eventually you will face the world with a smile that will eclipse any concerns. There is true freedom in showing the world the gifts that God has personally placed in each of us.

Let Your Light Shine for All to See

It's one thing to hide our flaws and fears behind a mask, but there are people who hide their greatness there, as well. Some people hide their accomplishments with a false-humility mask, because they are afraid of success more than they are of failure. I know that sounds crazy, but I've met people like this. They constantly downplay what they have accomplished. Consider this famous quote by Marianne Williamson.:

> *Our deepest fear is not that we are inadequate.*
> *Our deepest fear is that we are powerful beyond*
> *measure.*

Sometimes it is our light, not our darkness, that can frighten us. We may ask ourselves: *Who am I to be so brilliant, gorgeous, talented, or fabulous?* The answer is that you are a child of God!

We are all meant to shine, as the children of God. We were born to make manifest the glory of God within us. And as we let our own light shine, we subconsciously give other people permission to do the same. As we are liberated from our own fears, our presence automatically liberates others. That gives me shivers every time I think about it!

I'm not suggesting that you go around bragging on yourself all the time, but when the situation arises, it's okay to share what God has done in your life. The world is looking for people who are succeeding in life, because it gives them hope that they can do it, too. When you have a success story that arises from a dark background or situation, by all means share it to encourage others and to let them see the goodness of God working in your life. Let them know there is a light at the end of the darkness, and be that authentic light for them. I'm smiling right here!

Don't Be Ashamed of Your Upbringing

I recently heard Dolly Parton talking about the poverty-stricken upbringing she endured that inspired her movie The Coat of Many Colors. She said something that stuck with me:

> Don't ever be ashamed of your upbringing. That's just part of who you are. It may be a painful one or a glorious one, but whatever it is, it molded and shaped you into who you are today. It helped strengthen you to the next level of your destiny.

Even though we can never erase our past, and we certainly are not meant to dwell on it, we can learn many things from it. What the devil might have meant for our harm, God will turn for our good. Your journey is your journey, and no one else has your specific upbringing. Use what you have learned to your advantage, to be successful in what God has planned for you.

Statistics show that very few people these days grow up in a two-parent household; most are raised in a broken home. I can verify that fact from my years as a schoolteacher. One year when I was teaching fifth grade, I literally had one single student in my class who was being raised by both of his parents. I observed this regularly through the following years of teaching. Some of my students who were from broken homes went on to college and became very successful and professional adults, while others turned to drugs and crime. What made the difference? Some chose to follow their destiny and use what they learned from their upbringing for their good. Others developed a victim mentality, believing that society owed them something for their hardships.

I always say that people can become victims or victors, and the choice is theirs alone. I choose to be a victor. How about you? How will you turn the hardships or brokenness from your past into a tool for reaching your destiny? Likewise, how will you use the good from it, as well? Your upbringing is part of your authenticity. How will you embrace it today?

Being authentic means that you are able to express your inner self and become the person God created you to be. This is what I would imagine God saying to us when we embrace our authenticity:

> *I love you just the way you are. Don't change a*
> *thing. I put a lot of thought and imagination into*

creating you. I made no mistakes. I thought about your hair color, your eyes, your height, and your personality, and then I put tons of gifts in you, as well. Go use them all. Be all that I created you to be, and don't give any thought to what others think about you.

God designed you for a purpose, and it is His will for you to find it, walk in it, and achieve your highest potential.

WALKING IN
YOUR PURPOSE

The Bible says that God has plans for our life:

> *"I know the plans I have for you," says the LORD,*
> *"plans for good and not evil, plans to bless you*
> *and not harm you, plans to give you a future and*
> *a hope."*
>
> —Jeremiah 29:11 NIV

Our destiny is a journey, and we must walk in our purpose in order to reach it.

One Step at a Time

Taking steps one at a time is necessary in order to get to the next level of anything significant in life. The word *step* itself implies a process. Such steps do not make life harder, but they do create readiness in our spirit for our intended purpose.

I go to a gym quite a bit, and I often use the stair-stepper exercise machine. Even though it's my least favorite exercise while I am there, it does help me to achieve my next level of fitness.

God's purpose for our lives is so awesome that sometimes He must bring it to pass for us in stages. The word *unfolding* might be a better term, as He unfolds our purpose step by step, but nevertheless, it is a process that often takes place gradually, over time.

My mother used to tell me that my biggest problem was that I always wanted to know everything that would take place in my life far into the future. And I would love to say that by now I have finally "arrived" and that I never fret about my future, but honestly, I still do struggle with this issue. What I have figured out, however, is that although we cannot know what the future holds for us, we *can* discern the general direction that our lives will take. God will order our steps for us if we allow Him to do so. All we need to do is to take one step at a time.

First Steps

Everyone is at a different place in their lives. Some of us are on step number two, others may be on step seventy-six, and still others may be trying to discern what the first step in their lives should be. Believe it or not, some people who think they haven't yet found step number one actually have, and they may be much further along in the process than they thought.

So, how can we tell where we are and what our next steps should be? For me personally, I use a diagram of stepping stones. I like to draw a series of these stones on a piece of paper, then write down on each "stone" something that I have already accomplished that has moved me closer to achieving my destiny. You should try this, too. As you write out each accomplishment on the "steps" on your piece of paper, reflect on how far you have come in the process, and how God has helped you achieve each step in life thus far. You might not have accomplished everything you desire to complete yet, but by writing these things down, you will see that you aren't where you used to be, either. Add in a few steps that you think might be the next ones you should take. Your steps may differ from time to time, especially as the Lord leads you, but that's okay. Feel free to go ahead and change them on your chart if you need to. This visual aid is merely a tool to help you stay focused on your desired destination; it is not a set of limitations or a "map" of only one way of getting there.

Life can be uncertain and unpredictable at times, and your steps will likely change to reflect these fluctuations. Don't let life's uncertainty scare you away from dreaming big. It takes courage to dream big, but you can do it because you serve a big God who places big dreams inside of you!

Every new day brings a new adventure. Each day, when you awaken, set your day in order. Determine to put God first for that day, and your steps will become clearer as you follow Him. Try not to focus on how far away you still are from your destination, but instead respect where you are now in the process and celebrate how far you've already come.

God placed in you many gifts and talents that make you uniquely you, and He has planned great things for you to achieve while you are here on the earth. As you learn to develop your gifts and allow them to evolve over time, step by step you will begin to transform into the powerful and purposeful person you were created to be.

Encountering New Ground

Self-discovery is a never-ending process, and it leads us to encounter new levels of purpose in our lives. I find myself constantly evolving; by that, I mean that I am always discovering new things I like to do, and so forth. I also am realizing both new weaknesses and new strengths that I possess all the time, and sometimes I discover a new talent that I didn't even know I had.

When I was sixteen years old, a new restaurant opened in our small town. The owner asked my friend and me if we would like to work there, because he wanted young people to serve the customers. We enthusiastically agreed, and we began our new jobs the next day. Well, that day was quite a learning experience for me! I was able to greet and serve the customers in the dining room quite well, but back in the kitchen, I was a train wreck! I was constantly overflowing the coffeepot, burning the burgers, and I found myself in tears before the day was over. Unlike my friend, who did all of these chores with ease and stayed on at the restaurant for a long period of time, I lasted just that one day—and to this day, I have never worked in the food industry again! However, had I not tried that job, I would never have known about my weakness in that area. I had to be honest and realize that this was not a gifting that I possessed in my life. I had to be realistic and authentic when I encountered this new ground.

Tripping Ourselves Up

Regardless of what steps each of us is on, we will always run the risk of tripping ourselves up. Four main obstacles can get in our way: *passing the buck, playing the victim, comparing ourselves to others,* and *procrastination.*

Responsibility is a dirty word to some people, and their answer to this necessary aspect of life is just to pretend that they do not need to deal with it, in the hopes that someone else will eventually come along and take care of things for them. But when it comes to our purpose in life, this is not appropriate! God has created us to carry out specific tasks on this earth, and it we don't complete them, the terrible risk is there that they will never get done. *Passing the buck* on our purpose is *not* an option. If the responsibility laid out before you seems too overwhelming or it appears to be too much for you to handle, then try to break it down into smaller portions that you *are* able to manage in order to see your success take place.

Perpetual victims will always find reasons to blame others for their failures or their inability to fulfill their purpose. These people constantly make excuses for themselves; they may blame the economy, a lack of money or time, poor social connections, or even bad influences of other people. If you constantly feel like a victim, then begin to work on your thought life. One of my favorite sayings is this: You can choose to be either a *victor* or a *victim* in this life—the choice is up to you! Remember, however, that according to God's Word, you are *not* a victim, but a victor—in Christ Jesus!

Constant *comparison of ourselves to others* will cause us to stumble, especially when we think the grass is greener on the other side from where we are. Our purpose is just as important as anyone else's, even those who may have a national platform of influence. Each of us has significant value, and comparing our accomplishments is never an appropriate guideline for success anyway. What one person identifies as "success" will likely be different for another person. But if we are each fulfilling our own purpose in life and living our lives true to ourselves and to our God-given gifts, then we will be successful! If you are the type of person who is prone to comparing yourself to others, then surround yourself with positive people who will celebrate you and your purpose, and who will encourage you to strive to achieve it.

Finally, *procrastination* will always keep us from moving ahead in our purpose. If we continue to put things off today and always promise to do them tomorrow, then tomorrow never comes. And because tomorrow will bring new challenges, we must strive to address the ones that we encounter today.

Our purpose will set the path for our lives, and if we walk in it, we will find joy and fulfillment. All we need to do is take one step at a time, keep an open mind, avoid tripping ourselves up, and remain authentic as we encounter new challenges and levels toward our ultimate goal.

God designed you for a purpose, and it is His will for you to find it, walk in it, and achieve your highest potential.

AVOIDING THE ENEMY'S SNARES

Agendas and Opinions

Have you ever met someone who seems to know just where they are going and how they are getting there—and their passion about their journey is infectious? You know the type—those people who seem to be on a world-changing mission that sounds so exciting and that makes us want to jump on board with them and be a part of something bigger than ourselves? We all have met these people at some point or another and we may have fallen for their charm, ultimately finding ourselves knee-deep in their agenda to change the world or hanging on every word they speak as if it were truth.

Becoming sucked into another person's "grand purpose" can be a huge problem for many people. But our *own* purpose is just as important as theirs is, whether we realize it or not. We must always remember that there is no reward reserved for us if we work to fulfill someone else's purpose. We have our own purposes to fulfill, and we should stay focused on *that*, because people who live their lives on purpose will always be happier and more fulfilled.

Opinions are another thing that may entrap us and keep us from fulfilling our purpose. Every other person on earth likely has an opinion on what you should do with your life. It doesn't matter whether they know you or not, but only you and God have the true vision for your life. Other people do not know what you know, they have not experienced what you have, and they cannot see the desires you have in your heart. That is because God, not other people, puts those desires in your heart. Also, no matter how many times you may try to explain it, other people might never fully understand or appreciate your vision. We cannot let the opinions of others impede the fulfillment of our destiny, and so we need to be cautious in the counsel that we accept, always seeking out godly sources. Furthermore, we cannot allow others to prioritize the areas of our lives for us.

Rescue Missions and Other Emergencies

Our gifts and talents will always draw others to us, especially those who are weak or need help in the areas in which we are strong. However, I know of many multitalented and gifted people who become so distracted by other people who are seeking their expertise that they never have the time or energy to accomplish anything of value for themselves. They are constantly being pulled upon by others, and before they know it, so much time has passed—and the same people are still struggling and have not grown at all despite all the mentoring they have been given. I am speaking from experience in this area! All of us have probably had this scenario take place at some time in our lives.

I learned a long time ago that most of the people whom I desperately tried to help didn't really want my help at all. They just wanted my time and attention. Eventually I learned to discern those persons I could actually help and I focused my efforts on them while turning the others away. Please understand that I am not implying we should refuse to help people when we can, nor am I saying that our calling is not to help other people. There are many legitimate situations in which we absolutely must help others, but the issue here is discerning which people are truly trying to learn and better themselves, and which people are distracting you from fulfilling your own purpose in life.

While some people may be seeking your time and attention, still others are searching for a sympathetic ear that will hear them out and provide "helpful" advice. I say the word *helpful* here, because many of these people never intend to take your wise counsel and actually make changes to their lives; they only want to vent about their frustrations and problems.

One of the philosophies that I adopted a long time ago in my life was to refuse to allow my ears to become garbage cans! Yes, I will listen to other people talk about their problems and challenges when the need arises, but I don't allow people to dump all their problems and negativity onto me. I learned a long time ago that we can't change anyone—only God can change a person's heart. All *we* can do is point them to what the Word of God says concerning their situation—it is ultimately up to them to apply it in their lives.

We must use discernment when people approach us for our advice. One major red flag that someone is not serious about making any true changes is that they are not interested in what the Word of God says about their situation. That's definitely a red flag to me! Some people have laughed at me when I told them this, but it has been true for me: Some people actually do want to keep their dark lifestyles, but they also want peace while they do so, and so they want us to tell them that what they are doing is okay, even if it runs contrary to God's Word. We must avoid these distractions at all costs, because they will waste our precious time and delay God's purpose for our own lives.

Finally, there is a third type of person who doesn't want our time or our help, but instead consistently wants to drag us into their drama. I call these situations the "emergency-person distractions," and they usually involve close family members or friends. Some people will try to have us think that every situation they face is a dire emergency—and that we are always the solution to their problems. This places false guilt on us, and so we jump at this person's every whim and constantly embed ourselves in their mess. Before long, our life becomes their life, and we stop making progress in moving toward our own purpose. When we are faced with people like this, we must discern what a real need is versus an emergency need. Nine times out of ten, if you refuse to get involved, these people will quickly be able resolve their "emergency," oftentimes through some other victim whom they pull into the situation.

So, how can we stay focused when the people around us create so much drama? It's certainly not easy! It requires us to focus on our purpose, to prioritize our efforts, and to ignore any and all distractions that would drain our energy and pull us into situations in which we have no business being involved.

Too Many Balls in the Air

In addition to our everyday tasks, such as school, work, or family responsibilities, on average, each of us has fifteen other personal projects going on at any one time. These could include planning a trip, learning something new, reading a book (I'm reading three books right now!), or even volunteering on a new project. Most of us are busy people, and we often try to juggle too many balls at once.

Psychologists tell us that uncompleted goals will rattle around in our minds until they have been accomplished. This causes distraction from our true purpose. In one study, participants reported that, while trying to read a novel, they were constantly interrupted by intrusive thoughts about unfinished tasks. But when the researchers told the participants to make very specific plans to accomplish their unfinished goals, they then experienced fewer intrusive thoughts as they read the novel.

When we have too many balls in the air, we need to find ways to take some of them out of play. One way to do this is to make a list of our current tasks, and for each one, write out a resolution plan. This way, even if the task is incomplete, it will still be "resolved" in our minds, and it won't continue to interrupt our thoughts. Specific goals help us to avoid distractions.

Visualization is another powerful tool we can use. Thinking about the process of how to resolve a task will help our minds to focus on the reward of the outcome. For example, when I look at my cluttered closets, a thousand distractions come to mind, and before I know it, I've managed to put off the task of cleaning them for weeks. Sometimes I have to visualize clean closets, or I might never get around to completing that specific task, and I will continue to juggle it in my mind much longer than I should.

Isolation

Because it's almost impossible to agree completely on everything with any other human being, it is important to brace ourselves for the opposition we may experience when we begin to walk in our purpose. We cannot expect everyone to applaud our successes. On the contrary, we may find ourselves standing alone in our efforts.

The best thing to remember in this situation is that our purpose can never be fulfilled in isolation. Consider the world of nature. Plants use light from the sun and carbon dioxide from the air to sustain their life while they produce oxygen that supports our life. They produce oxygen for us, and we produce carbon dioxide for them. Both plants and humans have individual purposes, and yet they work together for the earth's overall purpose to promote life. Nothing on earth was created to function alone in isolation—especially people.

One of the enemy's most popular attacks is to get people in isolation and make them feel alone and useless. If our purpose is designed to help others, how could it ever be productive to stow ourselves away in a corner far away from everyone else?

One of my favorite sayings is this: God is really into families. He loves it when we fellowship with one another and use our gifts to bless others. The Scriptures teach us that God loves it when we fellowship not only with Him, but also with one another. He says that where two or more believers are gathered together in His name, He is there with them.[11] The apostle Paul put it like this: "For just as each of us has one body with many members, and these members do not all have the same functions, so in Christ we, though many, form one body, and each member belongs to all the others."[12] It doesn't matter if there are two people gathered together or two million, our purpose cannot be fulfilled in isolation. We all have something significant to give to this world, and we must work together to achieve it.

Stinkin' Thinkin'

Taking control of our minds is one of the toughest hurdles each of us faces in life, and it is something we will work on throughout our lifetime. It's normal to have thoughts of anxiety or doubt when we struggle with certain issues; however, it's critical that we don't dwell there. We must stop our negative thoughts if we desire to be all that God created us to be and if we are to fulfill the greatness that has been assigned to us.

If left unattended, our minds almost always lean toward dwelling on our self-doubt, our inadequacies, and our insecurities. For example, as God begins to unveil the great things He has in store for us, we may begin to shrink back away from what He is showing us, with feelings of doubt, unbelief, and a *who-am-I-to-do-this* attitude. The easiest way to stop such negative thoughts is to keep them from occurring in the first place. This requires us to proactively control our thoughts instead of letting them run wild.

Most people have to work very hard to keep a positive and upbeat healthy attitude. But I can't stress how important this is, because our thoughts will determine our attitude and the way we approach different situations in life. It also affects whether or not we are open to discovering our true selves. Consider this Chinese proverb and how it might ring true in your own life:

Be careful of your thoughts,
for your thoughts become your words.

Be careful of your words,
for your words become your actions.

Be careful of your actions,
for your actions become your habits.

Be careful of your habits,
for your habits become your character.

Be careful of your character,
for your character becomes your destiny.

—Chinese proverb, author unknown

Sometimes our stinkin' thinkin' (as we Southerners sometimes call it!) can get out of hand, and we need a total mind-set makeover. Changing old thought patterns is critical in order for us to reach our destiny. Our mind-sets can become locked into a specific gear due to events that took place in the past or our routine ways handling things. A person who is overcoming abuse, unemployment, bankruptcy, or any other negative experience must strive not to remain held captive by these experiences. Our experiences are merely life lessons; they are not the core of our beings.

If you need to create a "new normal" in your way of thinking, then start by researching every scripture passage you can find to learn what God says about you, then use it to replace what other people have said about you, or even what you've said about yourself. Speak those scriptures out loud, so that you can hear yourself say what God says about you. If you speak it forth enough, you will begin to believe it. I'm not talking about creating arrogance in your spirit, but rather forming a healthy image of who you really are in Christ.

Because we learn best through input via multiple senses, in addition to hearing yourself describe this new you and this new way of thinking, begin to visualize yourself as a new person, as well. I personally can attest to the fact that anything I have had to believe for first started in my mind. I had to speak it out loud, hear it, and see it before the thing became a reality. We will never become something we can't truly envision. For example, if you've always felt poor, then you must begin to see yourself as prosperous!

Reaching a higher purpose will require us to see ourselves accomplishing great things, even before we see any evidence of it coming to pass. See yourself in front of that large crowd singing, or becoming a bestselling author, or whatever else it might be that is part of your amazing destiny. Unlock your thoughts and let them fly; then you will begin to see yourself as the eagle, soaring high above the storms of doubt, instead of the chicken that is pecking away on the ground.

Once we shift our mind-sets, however, our work is not over. We must be vigilant to keep from losing ground in this area. When the enemy sneaks in and tries to tell you that you are insignificant, that you are unworthy, or that other people are more gifted and talented than you, refuse to listen to the lies. When battles come at me, I meditate on the Scriptures, declare God's promises over myself and my life, listen to inspirational messages, and sing and praise God with my voice. Doing this will set your mind on the things above and bring victory into your battle.

Ultimately, our purpose cannot be changed to fit our ways of thinking; our ways of thinking must be changed to fit our purpose.

Make Use of Your Mistakes

As we travel along in our purpose toward our destiny, we need to know that there *will* be times when we may stumble and fall along the way. The key to overcoming these times is our willingness to get back up and continue moving forward. We cannot allow ourselves to lie there in defeat and self-pity, and we certainly cannot start backtracking in our purpose.

Most of us use some form of global positioning system (GPS) when we are traveling. I use mine all the time, but despite its instructions, I sometimes miss a turn or take the wrong exit off a highway. When this happens, my GPS never calls me a loser or tells me to quit. It has never recommended that I just go home and forget about ever reaching my destination. Do you know what my GPS says? It simply says, "Recalculating." That's exactly how our heavenly Father speaks to us when we veer off our intended course.

God will never say things like, "You idiot—don't you know how to follow the directions?" or "Do you always make such bad choices?" or "Why don't you just quit and consider yourself a failure?" I know this may sound ridiculous, but that is actually how some of us think God responds. If you hear those kinds of messages coming up in your mind, know without a doubt that what you are hearing is the enemy trying to discourage you and cause you to give up. God loves us, and He will always encourage us to get back up and keep moving in the right direction.

He will simply "recalculate" our course in life, and show us how to get back on track with where we need to be.

Every wrong decision can be turned into a testimony, and every disappointment can, as well. Most of the greatest teachers I know have based their teaching on the mistakes they themselves have made. While it's important to share our victories in order to give other people hope, sometimes we need to share our mistakes, too, and make the most of them by helping others to avoid the same problems. In the event that they fall too, we may better be able to help them know hover ow to get up and start again.

We have an adversary that looks for opportunities to trip us up and hinder our God-given purpose. We must learn to sidestep his snares. When we stumble or fall along the way, we simply need to get back up and make the incident a lesson of what not to do—both for ourselves and for others.

God designed you for a purpose, and it is His will for you to find it, walk in it, and achieve your highest potential.

THE POWER OF YOUR PURPOSE

We know that the enemy is out for us and that he longs to thwart our efforts—but why? Why does he want to destroy our lives so badly? It's because our purpose has such great power to destroy his plans and strategies. As we fulfill our purpose, we will bring life to ourselves and others. We become a light for the Lord and we shine on the darkness, showing the captives the way out.

The Power to Change Lives

No matter what greatness or success we achieve in our lives that are a part of our purpose, if we fail to fulfill that purpose with love for others, it amounts to nothing at all. In fact, the Bible says that we could give all our money to the poor, or we could have a faith that moves mountains, but if we don't have love, we have accomplished nothing.[13]

Jesus Himself distilled the Ten Commandments down to two very succinct commands:[14] 1) Love the Lord with all your heart, mind, and soul, and 2) Love your neighbor as yourself.

Why is love so important? Because love conquers all. It is the most powerful force on earth, and it can unequivocally change people's lives. In fact, love is so powerful that it was the driving force behind God's sending Jesus to die for our sins and redeem us back to Himself. The Bible tells us that love covers a multitude of sins,[15] and that whoever does not love does not know God, because God *is* love.[16]

When our purpose is steeped in love, it has the power to forever affect people's lives—including our own. Jesus' life is the ultimate example of this.

The Power to Fulfill

When we are functioning in our purpose and fulfilling all that God intended for us, there is no greater satisfaction in our lives. However, the flipside is also true: A lack of purpose creates a deep longing inside of people's hearts that they will seek to fill with other things that can temporarily satisfy them—things like drugs, alcohol, promiscuity, pornography, and so on. Many times, substance abuse is actually rooted in a lack of purpose. When people feel rejected, insignificant, or useless, they often seek to relieve these feelings with drugs or alcohol. I wrote a book titled *Addicted to His Presence* about this very problem, and I would encourage you to read it.

Our purpose has the power to provide fulfillment and satisfaction with life that nothing else can do. When I think about this idea, I'm reminded of Mrs. Glover, who lives one of the most fulfilled lives I've ever witnessed.

The Power to Set Captives Free

Our prisons and jails are full of people who feel they have no purpose in life. I know this, because I receive letters from these people after they have read one of my books.

One letter in particular was from a man I'll call "Joe." It stands out to me because, according to his letter, Joe had been in jail for over five years. He wrote that he felt hopeless and that all his dreams seemed shattered. At one point, he received a copy of my book *Dreams Never Expire*. It came from a dear friend of mine who was distributing them as part of a jail ministry. Joe refused to read the book at first, because he had decided that his dreams had already "expired" and that there was no hope left for him. But after the book lay in his room for many weeks, he finally began to thumb through it. Despite his negative attitude, he reluctantly read the book, and he confirmed that it meant nothing to him. He stashed the book up on a shelf, thinking he would never read it again. However, he described a conviction that stirred within his heart to pick it up again. As he read the book for a second time, something began to stir again in his heart. Not understanding that it was the power of God working in his spirit, Joe began to weep. He hadn't shed a tear in over ten years, so this was very surprising to him. A few days later, he read the book a third time, and he decided that God hadn't abandoned him or forgotten him. There *was* still hope for his future. He began to feel that his past was dead, but that his dreams would live again.

When I wrote that book, I was just doing what I felt I was supposed to do at that time. I had no preconception of how it would affect my readers. I never imagined how a simple act of obedience in writing a book could have such a profound effect on other people's lives.

Our purpose has the power to set captives free, and I have witnessed this in my own life.

When we fulfill our purpose, it creates a domino effect, because our contribution to the lives of others helps them to fulfill their own purpose, and in turn, they continue this paying-it-forward cycle. It also creates a cooperative environment for those times in life that require people to work together in concert. Consider everyone who was involved in the events leading up to Joe's spiritual awakening. What if I had decided that writing my first book would be too hard, and so I gave myself a pass? What if my friend decided she didn't feel like visiting the prison that day and she failed to deliver the book? Had either of us failed to do our part, Joe could still be trapped in his hopelessness, whereas instead, Joe now understands that he has a purpose and he is on his way to a better and more fulfilling life for himself.

Joe experienced a life-changing encounter with God because everyone involved fulfilled their purpose. There are a lot of Joes in this world who need you to do the same. Don't rob the world of your purpose. Your purpose is important—and something or someone is waiting on you.

God designed you for a purpose, and it is His will for you to find it, walk in it, and achieve your highest potential.

YOU CAN DO IT!

The Bible says that we can do all things through Christ who strengthens us.[17] This is my favorite scripture verse. It reminds us where our strength comes from, and it is loaded with motivation for us that we *can* do all things. If you are wondering what "all things" includes, then I would suggest that you ask God what it means specifically for you. As for me, I choose to believe that God meant literally what He said.

Whatever we were born to do, we have been equipped to do. All the talents, abilities, and capacities that lie within us are just waiting to come out. Although the Lord has supplied the inventory, we have to provide the faith to use it and take the first leap to begin our journey toward our purpose.

Have you ever really thought about birds? Birds have wings because they were created to fly, and they seem the happiest when they fly. You can watch them soar across the sky and sometimes even hear a faint song as they fly past. It's no wonder that people put so much time into watching birds. When a bird flies, it's operating in its purpose, and when doing so, it becomes a beautiful sight. It's the same with us. As we flow in our purpose, we become a beautiful thing to behold, especially to the Lord.

An acquaintance of mine has a gift of prophetic painting that he didn't always know he had. One day in our worship service, he was asked to paint. Every eye was on this man as his paintbrush moved across the large canvas. People were mesmerized and the suspense was great, as no one really knew what the final product of this beautiful painting would look like. After twenty minutes or so, the man held up the most beautiful painting of Christ with the crown of thorns I have ever seen. Never having done anything like that before, he had stepped out in faith when he was asked to, because he understood that he could do all things through Christ who strengthened him.

So, what are *you* waiting on? For someone to ask you to do something related to your purpose? Well, here I am—doing just that!

People are waiting for you to pursue your passion so they can benefit from your purpose. Don't waste your time on trivial matters. God's glory and mercies are new every morning, and He's waiting for you to begin your pursuit. I understand that not every day is going to be perfect. Each day has its own set of challenges, and some can be unexpected. But by making your days count and not wandering aimlessly through each one, you will discover more meaning in your life. Drifting through life is not an option for people of purpose. Pick up the pace, and let's get going!

But what if you still don't know where to start? Then focus on what you can do *today*. I personally begin every morning with a great big "good morning, Holy Spirit!" Then I ask Him to guide my day and to help me be mindful of others. Don't worry if you don't know your purpose step by step yet, laid out over the next ten years in detail. Just start with today's goal of being a blessing to others at every opportunity you can find.

Believe in yourself and trust God to guide you on this path called life. Remember that God is for you and He is not against you. He wants you to succeed. Don't be afraid of either failure or success. When the time is right, you will be ready for what God has planned for you!

God designed you for a purpose, and it is His will for you to find it, walk in it, and achieve your highest potential.

About the Author

Beth Stewart realized the call on her life when she made a commitment to Christ at the age of seventeen. Her passion is to set the captives free through the truth of Jesus Christ and God's Word.

Beth is the founder of the *Triumphant Living* radio ministry, and she is the CEO of Beth Stewart Ministries, which reaches over thirty nations. A Bible teacher, author, public speaker, and radio talk host, Beth also holds a BA in education, an MA in education, and a BA in theology. She speaks to many church groups, conferences, businesses, and organizations in an effort to bring hope and encouragement and help to facilitate the fulfillment of destiny and God-given dreams within other people.

Dreams NEVER Expire
by Beth Stewart

2015 Readers Favorite Bronze Award

Dreams Never Expire uses real-life stories to prove that dreams can be fulfilled, no matter the circumstances. If you're looking for a sign to keep on trying, then you've found it here.

Addicted to His Presence
by Beth Stewart

Do you ever try to fill the emptiness in your being with activities, substances, or unhealthy relationships? If so, then this book is for you. Unlike other books that focus on the physical side of addiction, *Addicted to His Presence* addresses the spiritual side of addiction and gets to the root cause of the problem. The bottom line is that the only healthy addiction in live is an addiction to God's presence, and this book shows you how to find it and keep it.

EMERGE by Beth Stewart

About
Beth Stewart Ministries

Beth Stewart Ministries was birthed with a passion to reach a lost and dying world. Our primary goal is to win the lost to Jesus Christ and ensure their salvation. Our mission is to reach around the world to bring the Good News of Jesus Christ to as many souls as possible. Beth Stewart Ministries and its staff are accomplishing this through speaking tours, books, street ministries, and radio broadcasts.

BethStewartMinistries.com

Beth Stewart Ministries is a 501(c)(3) nonprofit organization. All donations are tax-deductible. You can donate directly via PayPal at info@BethStewartMinistries.com or mail your donation to Beth Stewart Ministries, 525 West 5th Street, Suite 334, Covington, KY 41011.You can also donate in various other ways. Please see our Web site for a list.

EMERGE by Beth Stewart

Acknowledgments

My first thanks must go to God for guiding me through this writing and publishing process, and for giving me the wisdom and guidance to see it through. Next, I would like to thank my wonderful husband and two sons for being patient when I disappear for hours to write. I am also grateful for Jennifer Minigh and her expertise and help throughout the book publishing process. Without her, I would not have been able to complete this process.

Review Request

I hope you have gained some helpful knowledge from *Emerge: The Power of Your Purpose.*

Now that you've read this book, if you enjoyed it, please let other readers know. Let's share the knowledge, helping other people to find their purpose, walk in it, and achieve their highest potential.

EMERGE by Beth Stewart

References

1 Jeremiah1:5
2 Psalm 139:13–16
3 Ephesians 2:10
4 "Authentic." Merriam-Webster.com. Merriam-Webster, Accessed March 13, 2017.
5 Exodus 31:3–4
6 1 Peter 4:10
7 Judges 6–8
8 John 4:1–42
9 Proverbs 27:21
10 2 Chronicles 32:31
11 Matthew 18:20
12 Romans 12:4–5 NIV
13 1 Corinthians 13:1–3
14 Matthew 22:37–39
15 1 Peter 4:8
16 1 John 4:8
17 Philippians 4:13

CPSIA information can be obtained
at www.ICGtesting.com
Printed in the USA
FFOW03n0112110917
39731FF